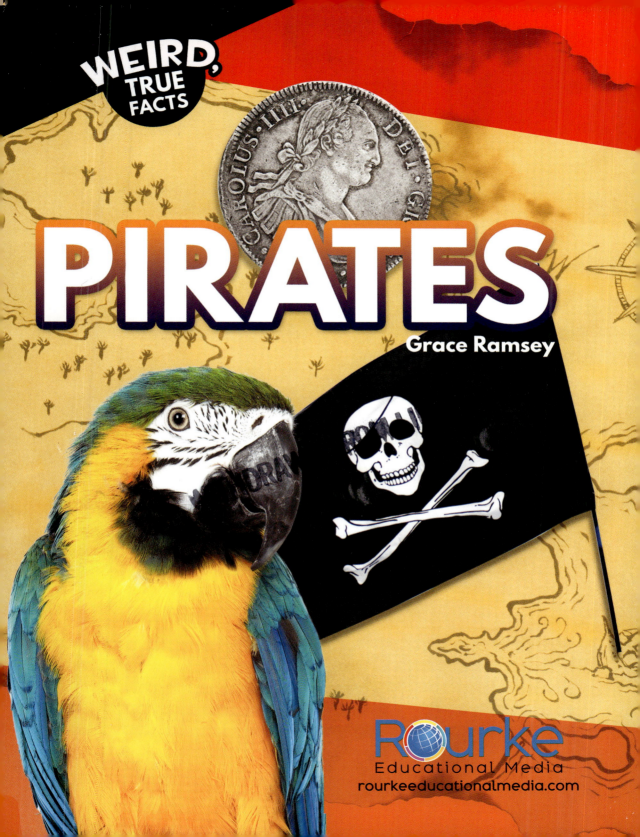

WEIRD, TRUE FACTS

PIRATES

Grace Ramsey

Rourke
Educational Media
rourkeeducationalmedia.com

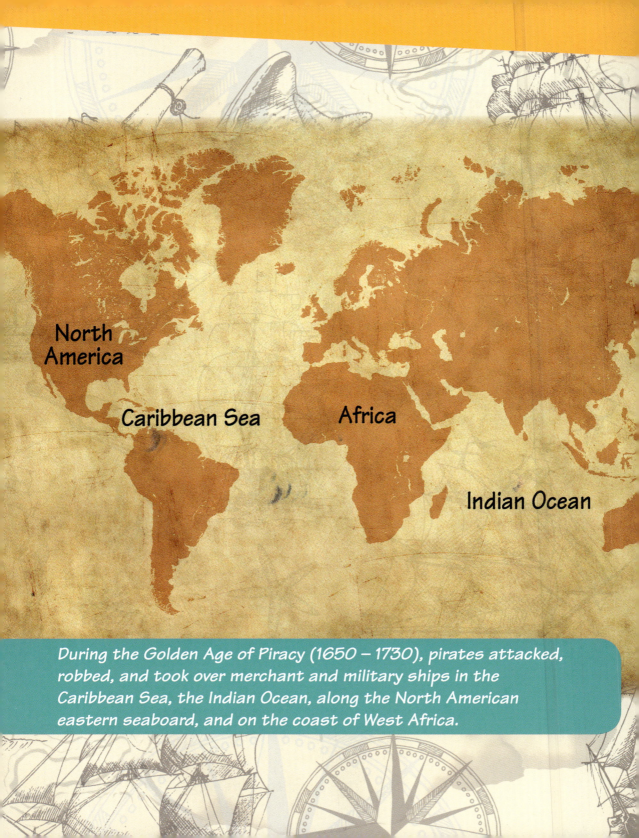

North
America

Caribbean Sea

Africa

Indian Ocean

During the Golden Age of Piracy (1650 – 1730), pirates attacked, robbed, and took over merchant and military ships in the Caribbean Sea, the Indian Ocean, along the North American eastern seaboard, and on the coast of West Africa.

Table of Contents

A Pirate's Life for Me. 4

Pirate Myths and Stereotypes 8

Pirate Codes and Licenses 20

The Jolly Roger 22

Famous Pirates of the Golden Age. 24

More Really Weird, True Facts. 28

Glossary. 30

Index. 31

Show What You Know 31

Further Reading. 31

About the Author 32

A Pirate's Life for Me

Avast, me hearties! Arrrr you ready to walk the plank?
Did you read that in a pirate voice? Pirates are popular characters in books, movies, and television. But real pirates didn't speak like pop culture pirates. They didn't bury treasure. And they didn't draw treasure maps! They weren't likely to make someone walk the plank, either.

Much of what we think about pirates comes from the ways they are portrayed in books and movies.

The Golden Age of Piracy

The Golden Age of Piracy lasted from 1650 to 1730. During this time, thousands of pirates terrorized merchant and military ships.

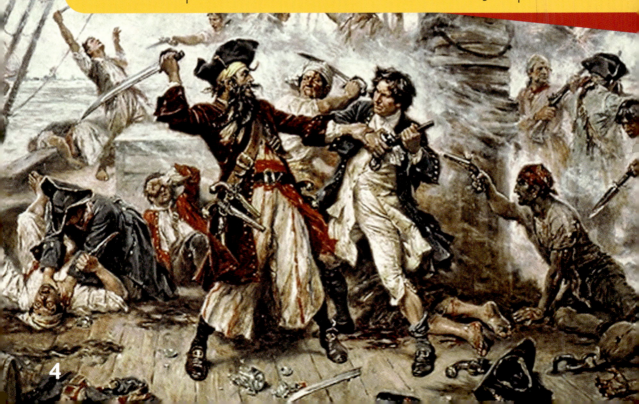

Pirate or Buccaneer?

A pirate is any person who attacks and steals from ships at sea. Buccaneers were 17th century pirates who robbed Spanish ships and settlements in the Caribbean.

Early buccaneers stole livestock and smoked the meat over open fires. The term buccaneer comes from the French word *boucaner*, which means to smoke-dry.

The Golden Age pirates inspired these **portrayals**. But who inspired the real pirates? Some historians say that was Henry Every.

Henry was a merchant sailor. Like many sailors at the time, he was given rotten food and cheated out of pay. Fed up, he convinced others to join him on a quest for riches. He seized a ship, sent the captain out on a rowboat, and set sail to **plunder,** pirate-style.

He and his crew attacked an Indian government fleet. Their loot of gold, silver, ivory, and jewels was enough to give each crew member 20 years of sailor wages. The value: About $200 million today.

Henry parted ways with the crew, took his treasure, and disappeared. No one knows his fate. But his exploits inspired a new generation of pirates.

Henry Avery

Henry Evory

John Avery

Long Ben

Captain Benjamin Bridgeman

Henry Every went by many aliases, or names, including Captain Bridgeman, Long Ben, and John Avery. Some now call him "The King of Pirates."

Fancy

Henry Every (c.1653 - after 1696) renamed his seized ship the *Fancy*. The ship was eventually either sold or destroyed in a storm.

Pirate Myths and Stereotypes

There are many **myths** and **stereotypes** about pirates. So what's the real weird truth? Avast ye, young freebooter, let's dig up the treasured details.

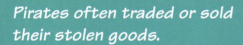
Pirates often traded or sold their stolen goods.

Buried Treasure

Pirate books and movies are full of buried treasure. But real pirates didn't bury their treasure. Not often, anyway. There are only a few reliable accounts of pirates burying their booty. Why? Because their loot was often food, clothes, and other goods—not gold and silver. Pirates didn't expect to live long, so there was no point in stashing anything away. Of course, since they didn't bury it, there was no need for treasure maps.

Walking the Plank

There are some accounts of real pirate plank walkings. But they were rare. And reliable accounts of the act are rarer. Flogging and marooning were common pirate punishments, though. And they may have tossed some captives overboard.

If pirates wanted to be especially cruel, they would tie their victim to a rope, throw him overboard, and drag him under the ship across the sharp barnacles. This was called "keelhauling."

Pirate Talk

Early pirates spoke in the dialect of their home region. They sounded like any other person. Linguists say our modern take on pirate speech comes from the movies—one actor in particular.

English actor Robert Newton (1905 – 1956) starred in *Treasure Island* in 1950, *Blackbeard the Pirate* in 1952, and *Long John Silver* in 1954. Robert had a natural West Country English dialect. Native speakers from this region of England emphasize their R's. They use "be" instead of "is" or "are." They also may say "arrr" for "yes," linguists say.

Newton's exaggerated dialect was soon mimicked in other pirate portrayals. And "pirate talk" was born!

Robert Newton as Long John Silver

Escape if You Dare

Daniel Defoe's 1724 book, *A General History of the Pyrates*, described ancient Mediterranean pirates holding a ladder over the waves, granting their captives freedom—if they wanted to swim for it.

Pirate Dictionary

avast ye – pay attention

dance the hempen jig – to hang someone

dungbie – rear end

hempen halter – the noose used to hang people

hornswaggle – to cheat

shiver me timbers – expression used to show disbelief

cackle fruit – chicken eggs

duffle – a sailor's belongings

head – toilet on the ship

Jacob's ladder – rope ladder used to climb aboard ships

poop deck – deck that is highest and farthest back

freebooter – a pirate

landlubber – a person unfamiliar with sailing

powder monkey – a gunner's assistant

Davy Jones' locker – death

ahoy – hello

blow the man down – a command to kill

booty – treasure

heave ho – a command to put some strength into an action

scallywag – a name used as an insult

scuttle – to sink a ship

seadog – an old sailor or pirate

Peg Legs, Hook Hands, and Eye Patches

When you close your eyes and imagine a pirate, does he or she have a peg leg? A hook hand? How about an eye patch? Many famous fictional pirates do. These are common pirate stereotypes. But did real pirates?

Limb loss was common during the Golden Age of Piracy. An injury or infection might require amputation. But of the known pirates, none has a missing limb. That doesn't mean unknown pirates didn't lose a leg or an arm. In fact, pirate crews often had injury insurance. Injured pirates weren't as useful for pillaging as able-bodied pirates, though.

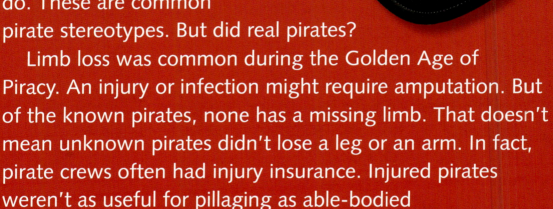

Disabled pirates were sometimes given less-demanding jobs on the ship, such as cooking and cleaning.

Wound Payments

Wound Type	Pieces of Eight
Loss of Eye	600
Loss of Arm	600
Loss of Leg	600
Flesh Wound	100
Loss of Finger or Toe	100

Pirate Insurance

Modern workers have insurance in case they are injured on the job. Pirates may have invented this! Some pirate captains guaranteed payment for injuries. A lost leg might fetch 600 pieces of eight. A lost eye might be worth 200.

Pieces of eight were Spanish coins. They were the world's first global currency.

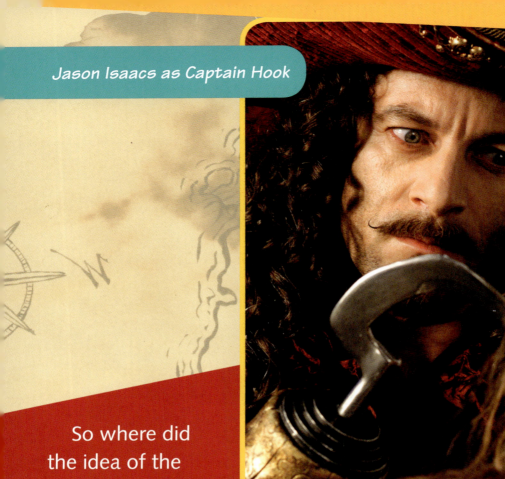

So where did the idea of the mighty peg-legged pirate come from?

Robert Louis Stevenson's classic novel *Treasure Island* (1883) features a one-legged sea captain named Long John Silver. In the book, he used a crutch. In movie adaptations, the crutch was traded for a peg leg. This popular character helped create the peg-legged pirate stereotype.

As for that hook hand? Thank another storyteller. J. M. Barrie's play *Peter Pan*, first produced in 1904, featured the fearsome Captain Hook.

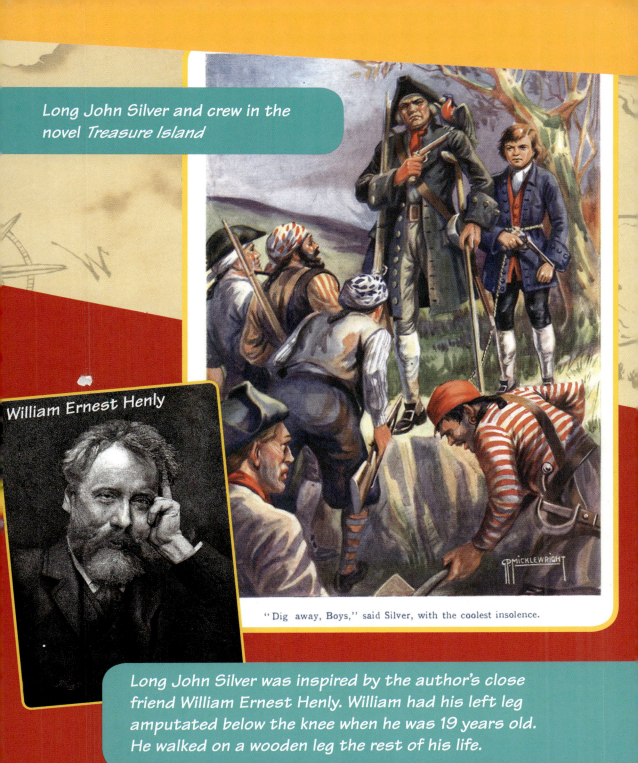

Long John Silver and crew in the novel *Treasure Island*

William Ernest Henly

"Dig away, Boys," said Silver, with the coolest insolence.

Long John Silver was inspired by the author's close friend William Ernest Henly. William had his left leg amputated below the knee when he was 19 years old. He walked on a wooden leg the rest of his life.

Fictional pirates often wear eye patches. But there's no **historical** evidence that eye patches were common pirate accessories. Some people think pirates wore patches to keep one eye adjusted to darkness for raids. They'd just swap the covered eye in the dark to quickly adjust their vision. The show *MythBusters* tested this theory. They found it possible. BUT! Some historians say this never happened.

We can point to *Treasure Island* and *Peter Pan* for peg legs and hook hands. But the origin of the eye patch isn't so easy to find. There are some accounts of real pirates with missing eyes, though. We just don't know if they covered them with patches.

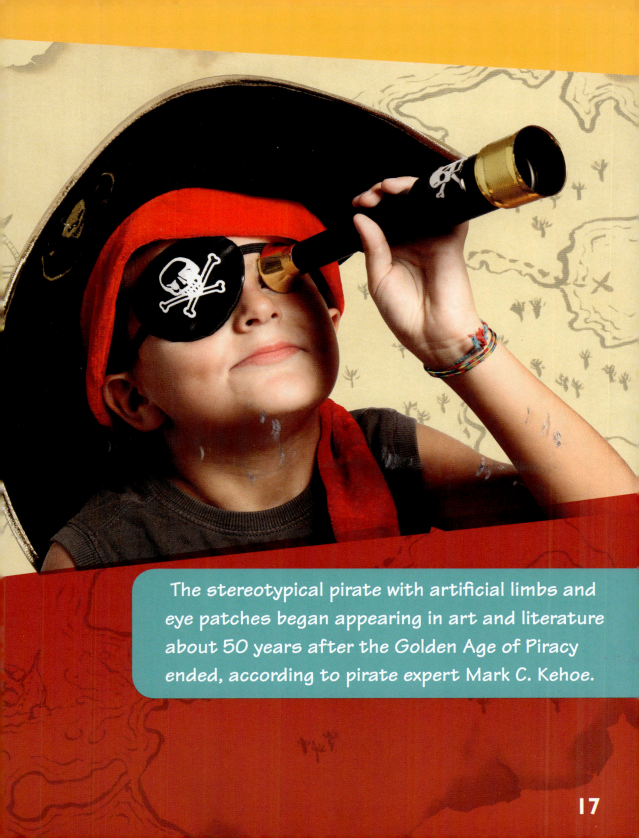

The stereotypical pirate with artificial limbs and eye patches began appearing in art and literature about 50 years after the Golden Age of Piracy ended, according to pirate expert Mark C. Kehoe.

Parrots and Piercings

We can thank Long John Silver's character again for making the parrot a part of pirate pop culture. But like other pirate **tropes**, there are no reliable accounts of real pirates with pet parrots. Still, historians say it's possible pirates kept parrots around. A colorful talking bird would've fetched a high price, so pirates may have stolen them along with other loot.

Pirates may not have worn eye patches, but they did wear earrings. For some, they were symbols of their travels.

Pirates charged with firing a ship's cannons may have kept balls of wax on their earrings to use as earplugs.

Earrings were also worn for superstitious reasons. Some pirates thought gold and silver in earrings could improve bad eyesight. Some thought they cured seasickness. Others thought their earring had protective powers that could prevent drowning.

The protective powers were worthless. But the value of a pirate's earring could pay for their funeral. Some pirates engraved their home port location on their earring so their body could be returned to their family for burial.

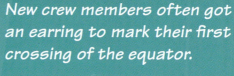

New crew members often got an earring to mark their first crossing of the equator.

Pirate Codes and Licenses

In the popular *Pirates of the Caribbean* movies, the characters invoke the "Code of the Brethren, set down by the pirates Morgan and Bartholomew."

Guess what? Sir Henry Morgan and Bartholomew Roberts were real pirates! And they were members of a group of pirates with a real pirate code of conduct. This code called for:

- An equal vote among members
- No stealing from other pirates
- No gambling
- Lights out at 8 p.m. nightly
- Always being battle-ready
- All disputes to be fought on land
- Payment for injuries received on duty
- Death for deserting ship

Be a Certified Pirate

Students at Massachusetts Institute of Technology (MIT) can earn a pirate certificate by taking classes such as sailing, fencing, and archery. The classes are part of the college's physical education requirements.

Excuse me, sir, do you have a license for that booty?

Some pirates had licenses to **pillage** and plunder! These pirates, called privateers, had permission to loot their country's rivals on the high seas. But, there was a catch: They had to share the booty with the government. British pirates preyed on Spanish ships. Spain and France also commissioned pirates to loot their rivals.

The privateers who sailed under England's Queen Elizabeth I (1533 – 1603) were known as Sea Dogs. These pirates carried a Letter of Marque from the queen, which gave them permission to engage in piracy against rival powers.

Sir Francis Drake (c. 1540 – 1596) was a 16th century Sea Dog. One of Queen Elizabeth's favorites, in fact. He stole from Spanish ships and ports, raking in loot worth millions in today's money! In England, he was a hero. In Spain, not so much.

The Jolly Roger

Pirates called their flag the Jolly Roger. Why? There are a few **theories**, but we don't know for sure. We do know this: The sight of a pirate flag inspired terror. And that's just what it was designed to do.

The sight of the Jolly Roger and the sound of a warning shot were often enough to scare up a surrender. This made work a lot easier for the pirates! It also kept the loot from being damaged in a fight.

Be Good to Your Crew

Sometimes pirates would ask a seized ship's crew their opinion of the captain. If the crew did not speak well of him, the pirates might beat or kill him.

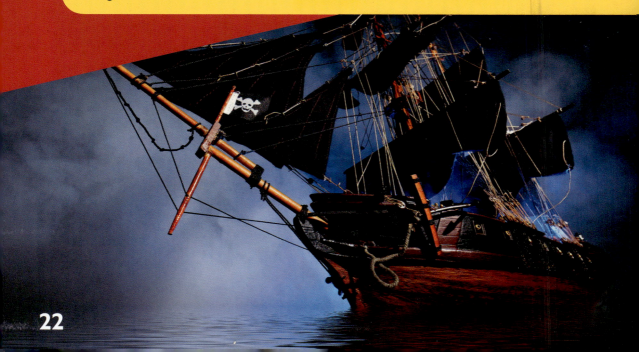

Pirate Flags

Henry Every

Christopher Condent

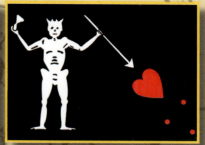
Blackbeard

Thomas Tew

Edward Low

Jack Rackham

Bartholomew Roberts

Traditional Jolly Roger

No Mercy

Clever Cover

A pirate ship didn't fly the Jolly Roger all the time. They often flew the flag of a nation, so they could approach a ship without raising any early alarms. When they got close, they raised their own flag.

Famous Pirates of the Golden Age

Blackbeard (1680 – 1718) was the most infamous pirate on the high seas. It's said he lit his long, dark beard on fire to scare enemies in battles. Blackbeard was known for his cruelty. Women who didn't give up their rings had their fingers chopped off.

Blackbeard was killed in a bloody battle off North Carolina's Outer Banks by the British Navy. His head was cut off and hung from the Navy ship. His body was thrown overboard. They only needed his head to collect the bounty! His death and the crew's surrender marked the beginning of the end of the Golden Age of Piracy.

Booty?!

The word *booty* comes from the word *bute*, meaning to share the spoils, or stolen goods.

Captain Kidd (1645 – 1701) took to the seas on a mission to hunt down pirates. Then he became one! He was eventually arrested, tried, and executed. His decomposing body was displayed on the bank of the River Thames—a grisly warning to other pirates.

Henry Morgan (1635 – 1688) was a ruthless buccaneer who led raids on Spanish settlements with the unofficial support of the English crown. In 1670, he and 2,000 of his men went on a mission to take Panama from Spain. Henry and his forces looted Panama City and burned it to the ground. Afterward, he ditched the crew and took off with the loot. In 1674, he was knighted by England's King Charles II. He was then sent to take over as deputy governor of Jamaica.

L'Olonnais (1630 – 1669) was a ruthless buccaneer. He took up piracy soon after arriving in the Caribbean as an indentured servant. Historians say he squeezed a cord around enemies' necks until their eyes popped out! It's said he also cut out a man's heart and took a bite. His cruelty bit him back, though: L'Olonnais met his demise when he was captured and eaten by cannibals.

Anne Bonny and Mary Read, known for their ruthlessness, fought side by side.

Mary Read (1695 – 1721) disguised herself as a man when she first took to the seas. She eventually joined Calico Jack and Anne Bonny on their ship. Mary continued dressing as a man, but her gender was known. She and Anne were known to be among the toughest pirates, never shying away from a battle.

Anne Bonny (1698 – 1782) left her husband and teamed up with John "Calico Jack" Rackham when she was 22. A woman onboard a ship was quite unusual because they were considered bad luck. But Calico Jack didn't care. Anne was fierce. Her shipmates knew she was a woman. She only disguised herself for looting and battles.

When the law caught up to the crew, most of the men were too drunk to resist. But legend has it Mary and Anne put up a fierce fight. Both women were tried, convicted, and sentenced to death. They were both spared when they claimed to be pregnant. Mary died in prison. There is no official record of Anne Bonny's death.

Women Pirates Post-Golden Age

Rachel Wall (1760 – 1789) was likely the first American-born woman pirate. She and her husband, George, disguised their ship to look storm-damaged. Then Rachel called for help. When a ship came close enough, the pair would rob it. They robbed a dozen ships and killed 24 sailors before their luck ran out. Rachel returned to land, kept thieving, and was eventually hanged. She was the last woman ever hanged in Massachusetts.

Cheng I Sao (1775 – 1844) was a prostitute turned pirate after marrying a pirate captain in 1801. For six years, the couple plundered the South China Sea. When her husband died, Madame Cheng took over. Cheng's fleet grew larger than many nations' navies. She created a spy network on land. And she developed a ruthless code of conduct. Deserters would lose their ears. Those who disobeyed orders would lose their heads.

More Really Weird, True Facts

Pirates were astronomers! Some of them anyway. Pirates who navigated ships used the sun, moon, and stars to help them calculate their position and course heading.

A drink called grog became popular among pirates in the 18th century because it was healthier than rum. Grog contained lime juice, which helped them ward off scurvy, a disease caused by a lack of vitamin C.

Pirates called someone who brought bad luck to a ship a "Jonah." Once marked a Jonah, he was tossed overboard. And if the bad luck continued, the pirates figured they'd fed the fish with the wrong man. Sometimes they would toss the accuser overboard to satisfy the spirit of the innocent guy they tossed first.

Townspeople often tolerated pirates' bad behavior because they liked to buy their stolen goods. These goods were cheaper than legally imported items.

Piracy isn't over. Modern pirates may not look like Blackbeard, but they are just as fearsome. Pirates board and highjack ships, often taking the crews and passengers hostage. Indonesia's islands and surrounding waters are among the world's most pirated areas.

Nearly all pirate ships were stolen. Once a crew took over a ship, it would get a pirate makeover. This included making more room for the sailors to live and making the decks stronger to hold the cannons.

Glossary

historical (hi-STOR-i-kuhl): having to do with people or events in the past

myths (miths): beliefs held by many people that are false

pillage (pill-ij): the act of looting or plundering

plunder (pluhn-dur): rob or steal things by force

portrayals (por-TRAY-uhls): depictions of people or things in plays or movies

stereotypes (STER-ee-oh-tipes): widely held but overly simple ideas, images, or opinions of a person, group, or thing

theories (THEER-ees): ideas or statements that explain how or why something happens

tropes (trohps): common or overused themes

Index

Blackbeard 10,23, 24,29

Bonny, Anne 26,27

code 20,27

Drake, Sir Francis 21

eye patch(es) 12,16 17,18

Golden Age of Piracy 4,17,24

Jolly Roger 22,23

Morgan, Henry 20, 25

Newton, Robert 10

parrots 18

peg leg(s) 12,14,16

Queen Elizabeth I 21

Read, Mary 26

Sea Dogs 21

Show What You Know

1. Who may have inspired a generation of Golden Age pirates?

2. What did Blackbeard do to scare people?

3. Why did pirates drink grog?

4. What did privateers do?

5. Why did pirates wear earrings?

Further Reading

Buckley, James Jr., *Who Was Blackbeard?*, Penguin Workshop, 2015.

Clifford, Barry, *Real Pirates: The Untold Story of the Whydah from Slave Ship to Pirate Ship*, National Geographic Children's Books, 2008.

Lubber, Captain William, *Pirateology Guidebook and Model Set*, Candlewick, 2007.

About the Author

Grace Ramsey is a children's book author and huge fan of pirate books and movies. When she's not researching and writing, you can find her reading and napping at the beach.

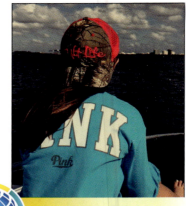

Meet The Author!
www.meetREMauthors.com

www.rourkeeducationalmedia.com

PHOTO CREDITS: Cover & Title Pg ©OHNGOMEZPIX, ©FlamingPumpkin, ©PetStockBoys/Alamy Stock Photo, ©TokenPhoto, Pg 2, 3, 7, 8, 9, 11, 12, 13, 14, 15, 17, 19, 21, 23, 24, 27, 28, 29 ©FlamingPumpkin, Pg 2 ©lukbar, ©By Regina Bilan, Pg 4 ©GL Archive/Alamy Stock Photo, Pg 5 ©1971yes, Pg 6 ©Anastasiia_Guseva, Pg 7 [Public domain]; via Wikimedia Commons, Pg 8 ©North Wind Picture Archives/Alamy Stock Photo, Pg 9 ©Howard Pyle [Public domain], via Wikimedia Commons, Pg 10 ©Ian Bottle/Alamy Stock Photo, Pg 11 ©forplayday, Pg 12 ©Kagenmi, ©koya79, ©tap10, Pg 13 ©FlamingPumpkin, ©Xacto, Pg 14 ©Pictorial Press Ltd/Alamy Stock Photo, Pg 15 ©Chronicle/Alamy Stock Photo, ©The Advertising Archives/Alamy Stock Photo, Pg 16 ©Elenarts, Pg 17By camilla$$, Pg 18 ©Lunnderboy, Pg 19 ©HighLaZ, ©evemilla, Pg 20 ©FrankCangelosi, Pg 21 ©National Portrait Gallery [Public domain], via Wikimedia Commons, ©Marcus Geeraerts the Younger, Pg 22 ©Neil Lockhart/Alamy Stock Photo, Pg 23 ©Orem, ©WarX, ©Fred the Oyster, ©Unknownwikidata:Q4233718, ©EugeneZelenko, ©Oren neu dag, Pg 24 ©Science History Images/Alamy Stock Photo, Pg 25 ©James Thornhill, ©Lebrecht Music and Arts Photo Library/Alamy Stock Photo, Pg 26 ©Lebrecht Music and Arts Photo Library/Alamy Stock Photo, Pg 28 ©Trifonov_Evgeniy, chris brignell/Alamy Stock Photo, Pg 29 ©FlamingPumpkin, ©By zhekakopylov, Pg 30 ©SongSpeckels

Edited by: Keli Sipperley
Cover and Interior design by: Kathy Walsh

Library of Congress PCN Data

Pirates / Grace Ramsey
(Weird, True Facts)
ISBN 978-1-64156-489-2 (hard cover)
ISBN 978-1-64156-615-5 (soft cover)
ISBN 978-1-64156-727-5 (e-Book)
Library of Congress Control Number: 2018930707

Rourke Educational Media
Printed in the United States of America,
North Mankato, Minnesota